ALLY THE ACORN HAS AUTISM
ALLY'S SENSORY OVERLOAD

No part of this publication may be reproduced, stored or transmitted in any form without the prior permission from Author

This book is about sensory overload and how it is hard for those who have autism to cope with all the different senses, such as sound, sight, touch and smell. It shows potential solutions for dealing with sensory difficulties, helping parents to help their child under similar circumstances.

Written by Claire Lamb.
Illustrated by David Lamb.
Thank you to those who have helped.

Make sure you look out for Sammy the Snail, Bernie the Butterfly and Buster the Bird.

One sunny morning, Ally and her mum walked to the park. Ally was excited to play on the slide and the swings. When they arrived at the park, Ally was skipping and jumping with excitement.

How many clouds are there?

As they walked through the park gate, Ally noticed a very strong smell. She said "I do not like that smell." So, she held her nose tightly closed and said, "Something smells awful."

After looking around, her mum pointed to a sign saying 'wet paint'. "I don't like the smell of wet paint," said Ally, holding her nose even more tightly shut.

What colour is the paint?

Once they were away from the gate, the smell was not so strong. So Ally decided to go and play on the swings. She sat on a swing, held the chains in her hands and started to swing. But not for long! "Oh no!" Said Ally. "This chain is too cold and the swing squeaks too loudly. I'll have to find somewhere else to play."

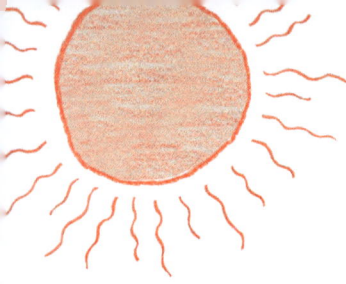

Ally looked around the park and saw the slide. "I know what I'll do," said Ally. "I'll climb up and slide down the slide." So Ally began skipping and hopping towards the slide. But as she got closer to the slide, the position of the sun made the light shine right into her eyes, causing Ally to squint, wrinkle up her nose, and cover her eyes. "Oh no," said Ally. "The sun is shining too brightly on the slide. I can't play here!"

On the other side of the slide, Ally spotted the roundabout and decided to try that instead. But, when Ally sat down on the seat of the roundabout, she sat right in a puddle of rainwater. Ally jumped right back up again, saying, "Oh no, I'm all wet. I don't like this feeling!"

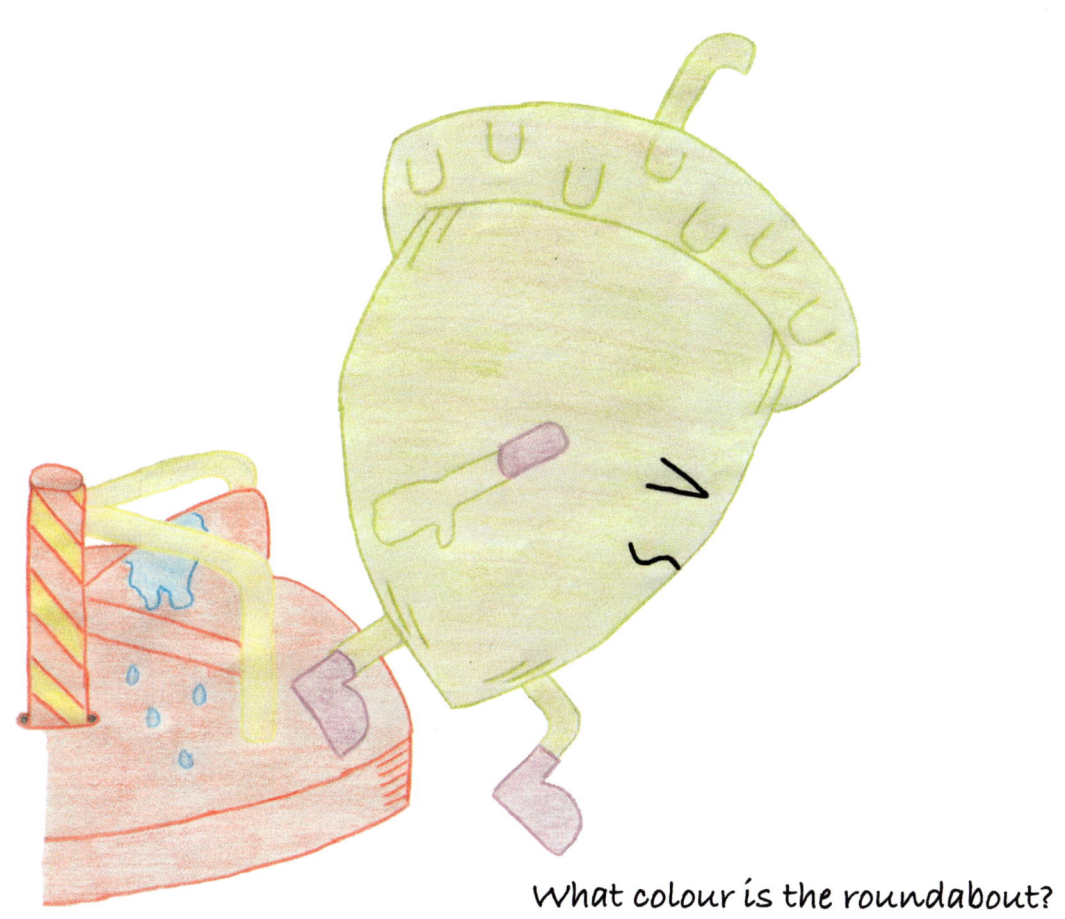

What colour is the roundabout?

Next, Ally decided to try the seesaw. Surely that would be alright, and lots of fun? Soon Ally was sitting on the seesaw, pushing herself up from the ground with her legs and then coming back down again. But the seesaw squeaked as it moved. "Ow, my ears," said Ally. "It's squeaking too loudly, I can't bear it."

Just then, Ally spotted the sand pit and decided to build a sandcastle. She picked up a bucket and spade, then began to dig and play in the sand. It didn't take long before Ally said, "The sand is all over my hands, and I really don't like the feel of it. The texture of it makes my hands feel rough." And with that, she jumped out of the sand pit.

What colour is the bucket?

Having tried EVERY activity in the park, and not finding anywhere to play, Ally became very upset and started to cry. Especially because a group of children nearby were running around and shouting to one another, and she had no-one to play with. "Everything here is too loud, there's an awful smell, the textures are horrible, the sun is too bright, and now there's so much shouting. I don't know what to do!" said poor Ally. To escape it all she ran to the farthest corner of the park and sat down by herself, feeling more upset than ever.

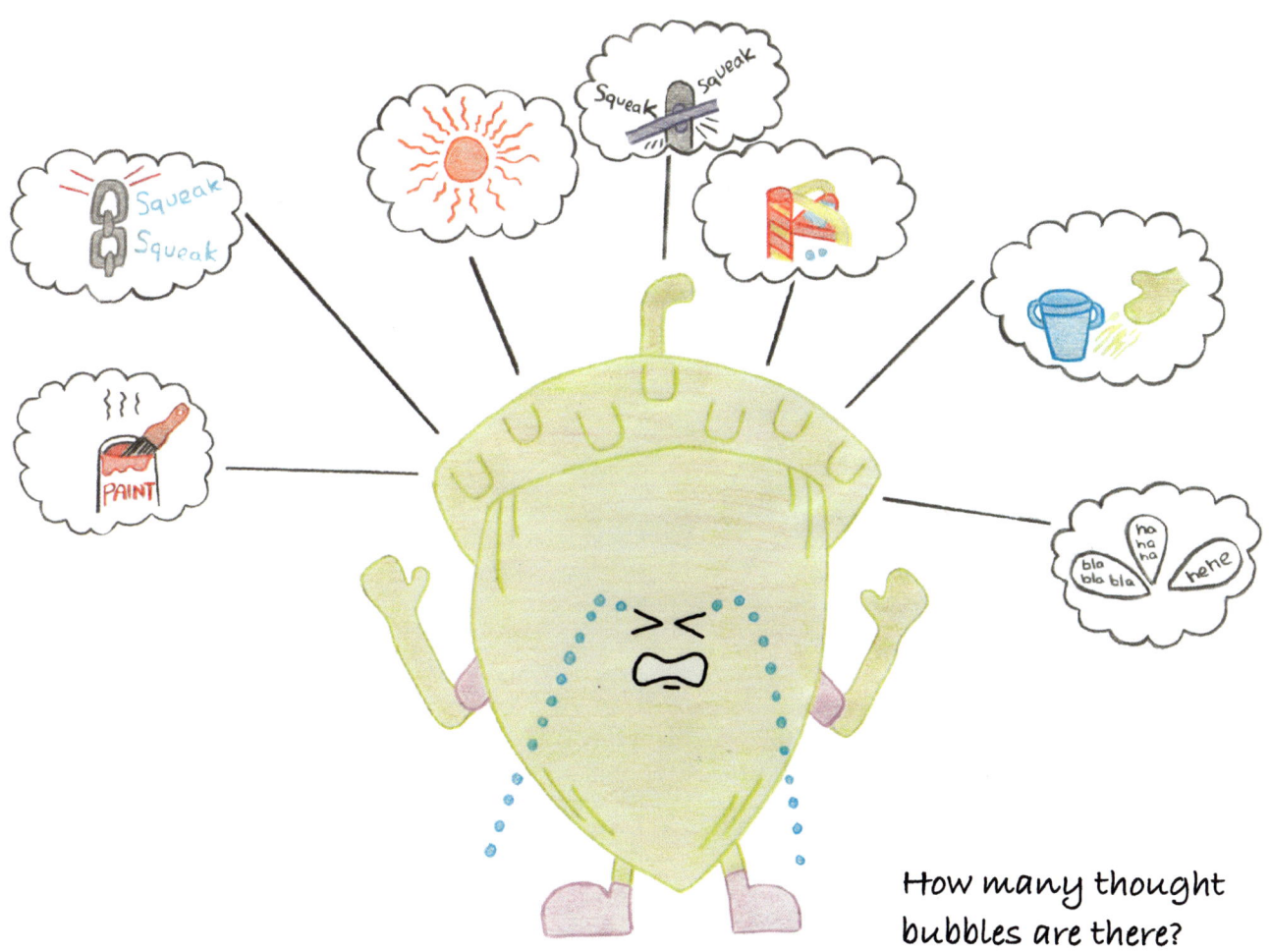

How many thought bubbles are there?

Just then, another acorn walked over to Ally and said, "Hi I'm Adam. I can see you're crying, you must be upset, but I can help you." Ally looked up at the other acorn in surprise, but also secretly pleased that another acorn was talking to her. She noticed that Adam was carrying a bag and wearing headphones. "I know what it's like to be sensitive to loud noises, strong smells, bright lights and different textures," said Adam. "I also know how to deal with them so they don't upset me anymore. Let me teach you!"

Point to Adam.

First, Ally and Adam walked to part of the fence that hadn't been painted. It was right next to a flowerbed of beautiful flowers. Adam said, "This fence doesn't smell of wet paint, so there are no bad smells here. Only the smell of these lovely flowers."

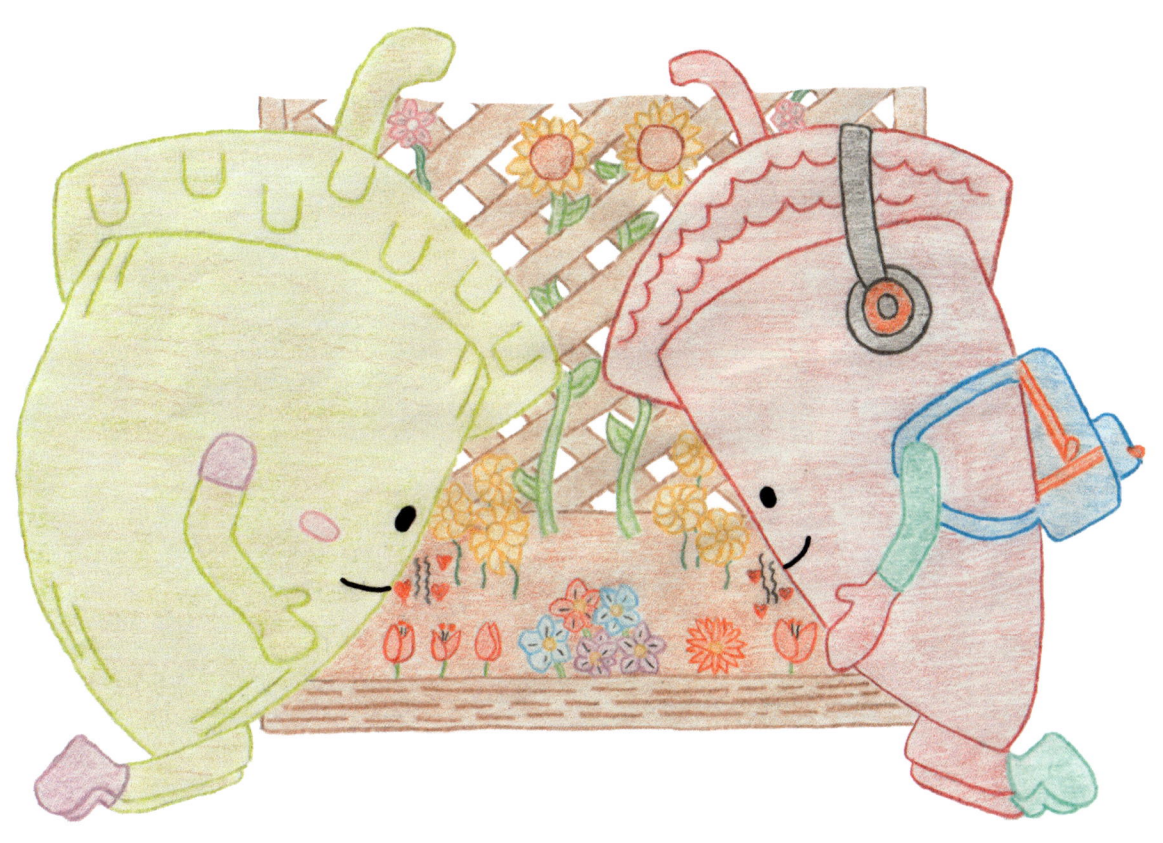

What colour is Adam's bag?

Next, Ally and Adam went to the swings, where they sat down side by side. Adam opened up his bag and took out some gloves and headphones for Ally to wear. "Thank you," said Ally, as she put them on. Then she held the chains and began to swing to and fro. "It's not cold anymore and I can't hear the swing squeaking. Thank you, Adam!" said Ally.

Point to Ally's shoes.

Ally and Adam then headed over to the slide. Before they got too close, Adam handed Ally some sunglasses and said, "Put these on." With the sunglasses on, Ally was able to walk right up to the slide. "This is so much better," she said. "It's not so bright anymore!" Which meant that Ally immediately climbed the ladder to the top of the slide, then slid down the slide. Again, and again, and again!

Point to Ally's sunglasses.

When they'd had enough sliding, Adam said "Come on, let's go to the roundabout!" As they reached it, Adam pulled out a small towel from his bag and helped Ally to dry the seat. "Thank you!" said Ally. "Now I won't get wet when I sit down." And she didn't!

What colour is the towel?

"Now the seesaw," said Adam. Before they climbed onto either end of the seesaw, Adam told Ally that wearing her headphones would block out the sound of the squeaking. He was right! Both Ally and Adam played happily, because they couldn't hear the loud squeak – not at all!

What colour are Adam's shoes?

There was just one last play area to explore - the sand pit. Adam said, "I wear gloves and use the spade so that the sand doesn't touch my hands. You should do the same." So, Ally put the gloves back on, and they built a beautiful sandcastle together. What fun it was to play in the sand pit without feeling the coarse texture of the sand on her skin!

Point to the sandcastle.

Ally had such a lovely time playing in the park with Adam. She was so happy that he had helped her find ways to cope with everything that had been bothering her. In fact, Ally was so excited about her new friend that she told her mum over and over about how Adam has autism too, and how he had helped her to block out the things that were too much for her senses. She talked non-stop all the way home.

Point to the clouds.

Hello friends. Which of these things do you not like in the park? Tick as many as you need to. Then think about how you can use the tips that Adam shared with Ally, so that you can enjoy the park, too.

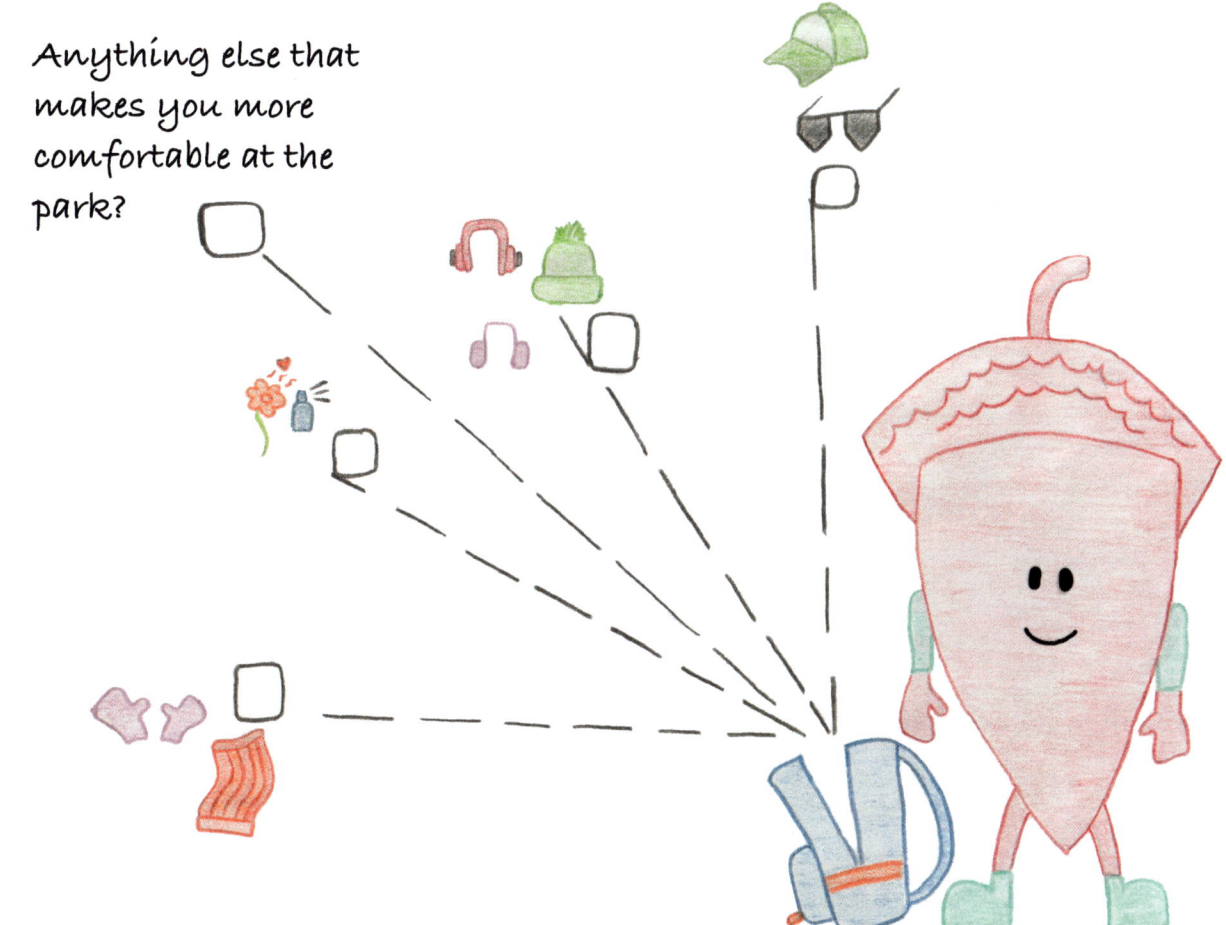

Anything else that makes you more comfortable at the park?

Printed in Great Britain
by Amazon